TALK WITH GOD...
HE WILL RESPOND

Contents

TALK WITH GOD...
HE WILL RESPOND

Patricia Hanson Enmon

ISBN 978-0-578-08985-0

The author's net proceeds from the sale of this book during the first year following publication will be donated by the author to benefit Cypress Assistance Ministries, Cypress, Texas. Cypress Assistance Ministries serves individuals and families in financial crisis, those on the brink of homelessness, the elderly, the unemployed, and anyone in its surrounding community who needs hope for a better future.

Dedication

To Kirsten, Hailey Ann, and John William...I trust you are in God's care and he has a plan for your lives.

8

Preface

You can have real dialog with the Creator of the universe. He wants to hear from you, he will respond if you believe, and it will change your life. If you have ever felt intimidated by the idea of talking with God, you will find prayers in this book written by someone like you for the times of your life when you need to get beyond that feeling.

Although I've lived most of my life searching for God, today I'm a follower of Jesus. I'm what was commonly called a "cradle Christian" (i.e., someone who is born into a churchgoing family, is baptized, and anticipated to live a Christian life). While studying religion at a church-sponsored liberal arts college, my religious beliefs were challenged. In brief, I failed to see God's mercy for his chosen people and, instead, focused on the killing and destruction of the idol-worshipping inhabitants of God's land of promise. I was also awakened to the fact that the world's population numbered fewer Christians than people of other or no religious faith, and I was in the minority.

I can't remember having previously been exposed to ideas that prompted questions to which adults I trusted seemed to have no answers that made sense to me—questions like:

- Why did God direct his chosen people to kill the people who previously occupied the Promised Land?[1]

- If people in most of the world's population don't believe that Jesus is their Savior, is God really a loving father if he condemns them to hell?[2]

- And, what about the suffering of innocents (e.g. the children suffering as victims of hunger, disease, slavery, and abuse)? Why does God allow that to happen?[3]

My religious beliefs were set off in a spin cycle that seemed to have no end. Initially, I searched for answers to my questions by exploring other religions—attending services and reading pamphlets or books about the basic principles of the particular religion I was sampling. After a while, I gave up and gradually admitted that I didn't have the answers to my questions and probably would never have the answers to them, least of all from anyone associated with a church (i.e., I was an agnostic.). Finally, I admitted to myself that I didn't believe in God (i.e., I was atheist.). Given my exposure to religion since childhood, it took real courage for me to be honest with myself about my beliefs and especially the lack of them.

Living a comfortable middle age, having been a health care executive for prominent medical centers in Texas, Oklahoma, and Mississippi, I had long moved away from my home town—far from my family of origin. I wasn't going to church or reading the Bible, praying, or consciously aware of a religious struggle within me though I had lived three decades of serial marriages and divorces at the time I finally responded to God's call to my heart. I was reading books in a series of novels when I stumbled upon the concept of God's grace described in the lives of the characters.[4] Although these books were well-crafted best sellers, they were about as challenging as a beach novel rather than scholarly reference books intended to stimulate the mind.

Incredibly, for the first time in my life, I began to understand the Grace of God. During a visit from my brother, who lived out-of-state, I mentioned my new insight about the concept of grace. A follower of Jesus Christ, he explained, "Patty, God is speaking to you. You're a baptized child of God. You may have tried to forsake him, but he has not abandoned you." That conversation was a turning point in my life.

Why hadn't God abandoned me? I knew it had nothing to do with anything I had done to please him. I believe I had hidden this truth from my heart: On the cross, Jesus had borne the separation from God that I had merited because of my arrogant defiance.[5]

I eventually began attending the church of my childhood faith, going to Bible study classes, and reading well-regarded books like those I have noted as references for this book. Gradually, the Holy Spirit brought me to faith in Jesus Christ. It was a struggle for me, and the most intimidating piece was trusting that I could really talk with God believing that he loved me enough to want to hear from me. I knew he was omniscient and aware of every secret of my heart, so I wondered why prayer was necessary. Now I know that God loves me, and he wants to have a real relationship with me. Our conversation together is important to our relationship (as it is to any relationship).

In talking with other believers, I have learned that feeling intimidated by the idea of prayer is not unique. Over a period of years, I persisted with prayer. In time, I began to understand that God not only listened to my prayers but that he was actually responding to them—not just *answering* them—but in dialog with me through events that occurred, Scripture that I read, thoughts that came to me, people who spoke to me.[6] It has changed my life.

This is not a scholarly text written by a theologian. There are many books written by scholars who are knowledgeable about the formats, settings, and forms of various types of prayers. Some of them are excellent for those who are interested in trying a different style of prayer. Some that I have read are cited in the Notes you will find at the end of this book.[7, 8] Unlike a scholarly text, this is a personal testimony with prayers written by one follower of Jesus, using straightforward language, intimately spoken with God as I've come to know him in a real relationship.

I don't believe in Jesus because I worry about being condemned to an eternity of fire and brimstone or because I want God to do good things for me now. I believe and pray because I know that God loves me, and I love him. I believe that he sent his Son to earth as a permanent sacrifice for those who believe. He is real in my life and has planned a future for me of unimaginable eternal bliss. I believe that this life is available to everyone who is a follower of Jesus Christ.

You can have a dialog with the Creator of the universe with simple words directly from your mouth, thoughts, and heart. He wants to hear from you in your own words, and he will respond. I hope and pray that this book will help you talk with God to enrich your relationship with him, to live the life God has intended you to live, and to inherit the eternal future he wants you to have.

Introduction

When I first became aware that I could really talk directly to the Creator of the universe, I felt intimidated. It's taken me several years to move beyond that feeling. Now I know that God doesn't want me to have anxiety about talking with him. I believe he wants me to talk with him in my own words, in my own way, any time I desire to talk with him. As it is in any relationship, conversation with God is a way to express the concerns, love, joy, sorrow, anger, gratitude, or anything that's important to our relationship at the moment we're talking.

Like any conversation, prayer is about two-way communication: I talk with God as he listens. As I listen, God talks to me. Sometimes I let my heart do all the talking and I listen. Sometimes God responds immediately; more often, I become aware of his response over time.

I found a verse in the Bible that has helped me overcome my sense of intimidation. It's most reassuring to me because, when I use it for my prayer, I ask God to accept my prayer just as King David asked God in ancient biblical times. He prayed:

> *"May the words of my mouth and the meditation of my heart be pleasing in your sight, O Lord, my Rock and my Redeemer."*
> (Psalm 19:14)

I often pray those words of David before I begin my daily meditation. It reminds me that even his anointed King David asked God for help with prayer. Surely he understands that I need his help and reassurance.

When we turn to the New Testament for help with prayer, we find that Jesus prayed. The Gospel of Mathew records what Jesus told his disciples about how to pray. He said:

> *"But when you pray, go into your room, close the door, and pray to your Father, who is unseen. Then your Father, who sees what is done*

in secret, will reward you. And when you pray, do not keep babbling like pagans, for they think they will be heard because of their many words. Do not be like them, for your Father knows what you need before you ask him." (Mathew 6:6-8)

Although there are times when we pray with other people, our Lord tells us we need time alone with God—not to pray long, eloquent prayers, but simply to talk with him. He knows what is in your heart, but he wants to hear from you. God, in the person of Jesus, says that very clearly. It may not be easy to find a time or place to do this but, if Jesus were in the room asking you to do this today, could you find a way? Consider this: Jesus is here now telling you that he wants to hear from you. It will change your life.

His disciples were not sure how to pray either, so Jesus gave them an example which we call the Lord's Prayer. It follows the New Testament verse quoted in this chapter and is found in Mathew 6:9-13 and Luke 11:2-4. It's a prayer I find comfort in praying as the last words I speak to God every night before I fall asleep. But, beyond the Lord's Prayer, what can one say to God? Jesus answers that question in the next chapter of Mathew in a verse that may be familiar. He said:

"Ask and it will be given you; seek and you will find; knock and the door will be opened to you. For everyone who asks receives; he who seeks finds; and to him who knocks, the door will be opened." (Mathew 7:7-8)

Jesus assures us that, when we talk with him, he will respond. If Jesus were here with you now telling you this, would you believe it? He is and you can believe it.

How will you know when God responds to your prayers? How does God speak to us? One of the ways he speaks most clearly to me is through his inspired Word—the Bible. That's why I read from it every morning before I pray. After reading Scripture, I try to clear my mind except for thoughts about what I've read. In the book of Psalms, we read:

Be still and know that I am God." (Psalm 46:10)

God will speak to us but we need to listen for his voice. God's voice is conveyed by the Holy Spirit as Jesus taught his disciples.[1]

"If you love me, you will obey what I command. And I will ask the Father, and he will give you another Counselor to be with you forever—the Spirit of truth. The world cannot accept him, because it neither sees nor knows him. But you know him, for he lives with you and will be in you." (John 14:15-17)

There have been times, when I'm on my knees in prayer and struggling with a concern I'm bringing to God, that I've been silent and sensed the presence of God with me in the room. Then, or maybe later, I'll find some clarity about this specific concern. Many times, looking back, I realize that God has responded to my prayer through another person, situation, or even an event that may occur at some point in the future. God may not have answered my prayer exactly as I anticipated, but the sense of fulfillment is so clear it seems miraculous—though others might call it a "coincidence". Although God's responses weren't so clear to me when I first began praying in earnest, over time I've found that I can validate his responses more frequently and with greater clarity. I feel a *knowing* in my heart that the Holy Spirit is active in my life.

But, what about those times when I'm troubled with something that prompts serious anger or anxiety and I can't even seem to talk with God about it? (A reading of the prayers in the book of Psalms gives some comfort to the thought that God can and will tolerate any amount of internal anger or distress when one is praying freely from the heart.) When I feel so overwhelmed that I can't even think of the words to say, I take comfort in these words from the apostle Paul:

"...the Spirit helps us in our weakness. We do not know what we ought to pray for, but the Spirit himself intercedes for us with groans that words cannot express." (Romans 8:26)

There have been times when praying that I have simply let the tears flow and could not speak, but I trusted that my heart was speaking to God in words that I couldn't even say.

In each chapter of this book, you will find Scripture from both the Old and New Testaments through which God speaks to us about the topic of the chapter. Although only an excerpt is quoted from xvi

Scripture, I urge you to find the suggested readings in your Bible and read a more complete reference to gain an appreciation of the context for the Scripture quoted.

The Scripture is followed by my thoughts about what those words mean to me. Although these comments are my own, they are drawn from a decade of sermons I've heard, Bible study, or books that I've read such as those to which I specifically refer in the Notes. As much as I'm able, I've tried to be faithful to Christian theology as I know it, but I'm not a theologian. I'm simply one follower of Jesus sharing what I've learned about God's Word as it has been revealed to me by the Holy Spirit.

My commentary is followed by a prayer to share with you how the Scripture inspired me to talk with God from my heart. Please remember that these prayers are not intended to be model prayers but only to illustrate how one person prays. God is eager to hear from you in your words, from your heart.

At the conclusion of each chapter, I offer some questions that may prompt contemplation. I suggest these not be used for the quiet time you have after reading Scripture and before you begin talking in prayer. That time is best left free from someone else's thought—a time to listen for God to speak to your heart. The questions at the end of each chapter are offered only to prompt further thought, and perhaps to talk over with God at a future time.

Although these chapters are structured in the way I meditate each day, this is not a book about rules for praying. Prayer is about free flowing conversation with God. No pretty words or specific structure is necessary or a substitute for your own way of praying. I find myself talking with God throughout my day. I know he hears and responds. I believe he wants to hear from you.

෬ONE෭

A Christmas Prayer

Scripture

<u>Old Testament</u>   Suggested reading: Isaiah 9; 10; 11

For to us a child is born,
to us a son is given,
and the government will be on his shoulders.
And he will be called
Wonderful, Counselor, Mighty God,
Everlasting Father, Prince of Peace.
Of the increase of his government and peace
there will be no end.
He will reign on David's throne
and over his kingdom,
establishing and upholding it
with justice and righteousness
from that time on and forever. (Isaiah 9:6, 7)

<u>New Testament</u>   Suggested reading: Mathew 1:18-25; Luke 2:1-20;
John 1:1-18

In the beginning was the Word, and the Word was with God, and the Word was God. He was with God in the beginning.

Through him all things were made; without him nothing was made that has been made. In him was life, and that life was the light of men.

The Word became flesh and made his dwelling among us.

(John 1:1-4, 14)

What does this Scripture mean to me?

The Old Testament gives an account of God's covenant with his chosen people. Even though they were chosen to inherit the Promised Land, the narrative is replete with cycles of rebellion and infidelity in their relationship with God. His steadfast love for them—calling them back and redeeming them again and again—is the counterpoint to this rich story. Although God was their king, they longed for an earthly king like the neighboring kingdoms.[1] Although he warned them of the dangers, God relented.[2] Through his prophet, Samuel, he anointed their first king, Saul, followed by the shepherd boy, David. David grew to be a man of strength and passion and, like all human beings, was capable of great sin. But he had a unique relationship with God because, above all, he had complete trust in God to redeem him and guide him to lead the nation of God's chosen people.

More than 200 years after the reign of King David, God spoke to his people through these impassioned writings of the prophet Isaiah who foretold that it would be through David's lineage that the Messiah would be born to establish a new covenant, with people of all nations, that would last forever. It was a message of hope for God's chosen people before they were exiled into captivity by foreign invaders. In the book of Isaiah, the tenth chapter, we read that those who remained faithful to God were referred to as a "remnant" (i.e., survivors).[3] Isaiah prophesied in the eleventh chapter referring to the Messiah as "A shoot...from the stump of Jesse" (which refers to the legacy of King David, the son of Jesse and the forebear of Jesus, the Messiah).[4]

The Christmas story most familiar to many people is found in the second chapter of the Gospel of Luke. It records the familiar story of the Virgin Mary giving birth to a baby boy, wrapping him in cloth and laying him in a manger in the town of Bethlehem, known as the town of David. Luke tells the story with beautiful imagery of an angel of the Lord making the first announcement—the birth of the long-awaited Messiah—to humble shepherds in the fields. As any of us would likely react, the shepherds were amazed and hurried to Bethlehem to see the baby. Luke tells us that, when they left, they spread the word that they had been told by an angel of God that the Messiah had been born. That story has captivated the imagination of people for all time so powerfully that, millennia later, the birth of Jesus is celebrated as Christmas throughout the world.

The Gospel of Mathew gives another rendering of the story told by Luke. Mathew connects the birth of Jesus to the Old Testament prophesy of the Messiah with the use of the name, "…Immanuel—which means 'God with us'."[5] It's this concept that John was able to crystallize in his explanation of the Christmas story.

The apostle John, known to have been especially close to Jesus, told another version of the Christmas story that is even more awesome than that described in either Luke or Mathew.[6] In this version, God speaks to us with no embellishment: He offers no explanation of virgin birth, no picturesque pastoral scene of shepherds watching their sheep in the hills surrounding an ancient village, no glorious choirs of angels making an astonishing announcement that the Messiah had been born. Nevertheless, John's words are exceptionally clear and compelling. He wrote that the Word was with God in the beginning and that in him was life that was sent as light for all people. The Word he described became human in Jesus, who we know to be the fulfillment of God's promise as Isaiah prophesied.

John discerned an essential truth of Christmas: Before time began, Jesus was God. In the third chapter of John, we learn God's purpose for coming to earth as a human infant. We read:

> *"For God so loved the world that he gave his one and only Son, that whoever believes in him shall not perish but have eternal life."* (John 3:16)

This is the miracle of miracles—God's eloquent message for Christmas recorded by his servant, John.

Prayer

Lord God,

As I celebrate Christmas, I want my heart to be focused on the miracle you have given the world through the birth of Jesus. In previous years, my mind was distracted with a flurry of shopping, decorating, and trivial preparation. (Think about specific distractions and ask God to relieve you of this burden.) I know that you sent your Son, Jesus Christ, to the world as a human baby, that his life was your gift to me, and that his life is the light that can shine in my own life. Thank you for sending your own Son to rescue me from the arrogant defiance that had filled my heart. Fill my heart with peace and joy knowing that Jesus is my Lord and Savior. In his name I pray. Amen

Questions to Consider

- What's so important about the connection of the lineage of King David and the birth of Jesus?

- To what was the apostle John referring as "the Word"?

- Why might God have chosen to send Christ, the Messiah, to earth as a human baby?

- Would refocusing the celebration of Christmas on the birth of Jesus be helpful to you?

- If you want to refocus your celebration of Christmas, how could prayer help you?

ೞTWOಎ

A Prayer for Guidance

Scripture

<u>Old Testament</u>   Suggested reading: Jeremiah 29:1-19

"For I know the plans I have for you," declares the Lord, "plans to prosper you and not to harm you, plans to give you hope and a future. Then you will call upon me and come and pray to me, and I will listen to you. You will seek me and find me when you seek me with all your heart." (Jeremiah 29:11-13)

<u>New Testament</u>   Suggested reading: Mathew 11:16-30

"Come to me, all you who are weary and burdened, and I will give you rest. Take my yoke upon you and learn from me, for I am gentle and humble in heart, and you will find rest for your souls. For my yoke is easy and my burden is light." (Mathew 11:28-30)

What does this Scripture mean to me?

A reading of the book of Jeremiah reveals God speaking to his chosen people about his judgment for their unfaithfulness—the invasion and destruction of Jerusalem as they are banished to Babylon. The Scripture above quotes from a letter God's prophet, Jeremiah, sent to those who were exiled. The letter brought a message of hope and encouraged God's people to prosper in their exile. It confirmed that the exile was no accident, and God had not abandoned them. God spoke through Jeremiah to give them direction for his sovereign plan for their future. He asked them to pray to him, and he would listen if they opened their hearts to him and honestly sought him.

Notice that there was no hesitation or ambivalence in Jeremiah's letter. He was confident that he was speaking about God's own plan for his chosen people. Jeremiah was a prophet who wrote in poetry with vivid imagery; yet, he didn't mince words. In further reading of this chapter, he described the people of Judah who stayed behind, after the people of Jerusalem were exiled, as rotten fruit because they didn't listen to him. And, he reminded those in exile that they didn't listen either. Unrighteousness abounded but, once again, God offered them his grace and gave his chosen people another opportunity to obediently follow his plan for their future.

When we turn to the words of Jesus from the Gospel of Mathew, we read his description of more unfaithfulness—more unwillingness of the Jewish establishment to accept the truth of his mission. Jesus spoke these words in the context of his lament about the cities in which he performed miracles to no avail. Jesus' words seem to echo the reproach God spoke through Jeremiah.

The joy we can take from this passage is his message to his followers. Like his Father, Jesus confirmed the sovereign nature of God's plan for his new covenant. He described the condition of obediently living the life God has planned for us as a "yoke". He invites us to take it upon us and learn of his plan for us. His yoke is not oppressive. He promised to be gentle and to help us with the burden. Lest we think of this life accepting a yoke from Jesus as difficult and boring, remember that Jesus was no dull human being but the charismatic Son of God. This is his invitation to live an empowered righteous life, not through our own efforts, but because we accept his yoke. The righteousness of this is not of our own doing but from the direction we accept from the Holy Spirit who he sent to guide us. (Note that there is a difference between being self-righteous and accepting the yoke from Jesus to live the righteous life God has planned for us.)[1]

In the various roles we have in our lives—whether parents of children who need our guidance, friends of those who are also trying to discern God's plan for their lives, leaders in our communities trying to understand how to serve God's calling to provide leadership, members of a church who want to bring the love of Jesus to worship and discipleship, or simply one follower of Jesus Christ eager to live the life God has ordained for each of us—the only viable option is to bring our concerns to God. Jesus has promised that, if we accept his yoke, he will guide us. It's no more simple or complex than that.

During times when we're struggling with daily concerns or an ethical dilemma or a major decision in the course of our life, God is there for us. He will listen to our prayers if we open our heart to him. He invites us to trust him completely, and he will help each of us discern his direction for our life. Jesus will guide us along the pathway he has charted for our lives and help us carry the burdens along the way.

Prayer

Lord Jesus,

I come to you on my knees to ask you for guidance. I'm feeling confused. (Describe the concerns that are troubling you.) I know you love me and that you have a plan for my life. Help me to take on your yoke and open my heart to receive the guidance of your Holy Spirit. I pray for strength of faith to hear your response and follow your guidance. Help me trust your encouraging words that you will help me with my burdens. In your name I pray. Amen

Questions to Consider

- Could God have been speaking to you through the words of Jeremiah?

- How do you feel about the description of God's sovereign plan for your life as a "yoke"?

- Are you willing to accept the yoke to have his powerful help with your burdens as well as the joy of serving him?

- Will you open your heart to discern his guidance?

- How can you support God's plan for the people you love?

❧THREE❧

A Prayer for Faith

Scripture

<u>Old Testament</u>   Suggested reading: Genesis 22:1-18

Some time later God tested Abraham. He said to him, "Abraham!"

"Here I am," he replied.

Then God said, "Take your son, your only son, Isaac, whom you love, and go to the region of Moriah. Sacrifice him there as a burnt offering on one of the mountains I will tell you about."

When they reached the place God had told him about, Abraham built an altar and arranged the wood on it. He bound his son Isaac and laid him on the altar, on top of the wood. Then he reached out his hand and took the knife to slay his son. But the angel of the Lord called out to him from heaven, "Abraham, Abraham!"

"Here I am," he replied.

"Do not lay a hand on the boy," he said. "Do not do anything to him. Now I know that you fear God, because you have not withheld from me your son, your only son."

Abraham looked up and there in a thicket he saw a ram caught by its horns. He went over and took the ram and sacrificed it as a burnt offering instead of his son. So Abraham called that place The Lord Will Provide. And to this day it is said, "On the mountain of the Lord it will be provided."

The angel of the Lord called Abraham from heaven a second time and said, "I swear by myself, declares the Lord, that because you have done this and have not withheld your son, your only son, I will surely bless you and make your descendents as numerous as the stars in the sky and as the sand on the seashore. Your descendents will take possession of the cities of their enemies, and through your offspring all nations on earth will be blessed, because you have obeyed me." (Genesis 22: 1-2, 9-18)

<u>New Testament</u>   Suggested reading: Mark 9:2-29

A man in the crowd answered, "Teacher, I brought you my son, who is possessed by a spirit that has robbed him of speech. Whenever it seizes him, it throws him to the ground. He foams at the mouth, gnashes his teeth and becomes rigid. I asked your disciples to drive out the spirit, but they could not."

"O unbelieving generation," Jesus replied, "how long shall I stay with you? How long shall I put up with you? Bring the boy to me."

So they brought him. When the spirit saw Jesus, it immediately threw the boy into a convulsion. He fell to the ground and rolled around, foaming at the mouth.

Jesus asked the boy's father, "How long has he been like this?"

"From childhood," he answered. "It has often thrown him into fire or water to kill him. But if you can do anything, take pity on us and help us."

" 'If you can'?" said Jesus. "Everything is possible for him who believes."

Immediately the boy's father exclaimed, "I do believe; help me overcome my unbelief!"

When Jesus saw that a crowd was running to the scene, he rebuked the evil spirit. "You deaf and mute spirit," he said, "I command you, come out of him and never enter him again."

The spirit shrieked, convulsed him violently and came out. The boy looked so much like a corpse that many said, "He's dead." But Jesus took him by the hand and lifted him to his feet and he stood up.

After Jesus had gone indoors, his disciples asked him privately, "Why couldn't we drive it out?"

He replied, "This kind can come out only by prayer." (Mark 9:17-29)

What does this Scripture mean to me?

Two fathers, two prayers: One was a prayer lived by a man to whom God spoke through an angel, a man of such strong trust in God that he was willing to sacrifice his beloved son; the other was by a man with faith so fragile he needed help from Jesus to overcome his lack of trust as he pleaded with him to heal his son. Today Abraham's response seems shocking. If God speaks to us through prayer, the thought of receiving this kind of message is enough to think about whether a life of prayer is what we really want!

How could God demand that Abraham sacrifice his own son? Almost as soon as this question emerges, we have a glimmer of its fundamental absurdity. This story seems emblematic of God's new covenant as an image of Jesus nailed to the cross comes into view in our mind's eye, and we realize that God would know the pain of sacrificing one's own son. But why would God, who later commanded the Israelites to abstain from sacrificing their children as did their idol-worshiping neighbors, ask Abraham to sacrifice his son Isaac?[1] God knew Abraham to be a man of faith, but he was also testing his obedience before making a promise to him that he would be the father of the whole nation of his chosen people and all believers who would come after them. This was no inconsequential promise. It was the beginning of God's plan to lay claim to all of his children of every nation on earth for all time—to offer them an inheritance in his eternal kingdom if they would trust in him as God.

In striking contrast to Abraham's strong faith, we read about the desperate father in Mark's Gospel. His son had suffered with seizures since childhood. He had heard about the teacher from Nazareth who could heal the sick. He encountered nine of Jesus' disciples in the foothills of Mount Hermon. When he learned that Jesus wasn't there, he asked the disciples to drive the evil spirit from his son to stop the seizures. Their failure led to arguing between the disciples and the teachers of the law who were in the crowd.

Jesus, accompanied by Peter, James, and John, came upon this scene after his transfiguration on the mountain.[2] There, in view of these disciples, Jesus was revealed by God to be his Son. For the disciples who accompanied him, it must have been a powerful experience beyond our imagination. Coming upon this disruptive scene as they returned, Jesus was prompted to say aloud to the nine disciples there, "How long shall I put up with you?"[3] It seems almost as if he was reproving them as one would scold children.

When they brought the boy to him, Jesus asked the boy's father how long he had been in this condition. When the man answered, he appealed to Jesus to help them, "If you can do anything..."[4]

" 'If you can'?" said Jesus repeating the anguished father's words which he followed by this reassurance, "Everything is possible for him who believes."[5]

The man immediately exclaimed, "I do believe; help me overcome my unbelief."[6] It was a prayer spoken directly to Jesus. Jesus responded immediately and healed his son.

When his disciples asked why they had not been able to heal the boy, Jesus reminded them that only prayer could heal—that they had no power over demonic spirits on their own. Healing of this boy could only be accomplished by appealing to God.

Like the father in this story, we may all have times when we have doubted our faith. We believe, but we long for a stronger faith. Faith is a gift from God which he gives to us, not because we deserve it, but because he wants us to have it. We have only to open our heart and, believing he will respond, ask.

Prayer

Lord God,

Thank you for calling me to you and awakening my heart to your generous love for me. (Tell God how you are aware of his love in your life.) I long for stronger faith in the saving grace of your Son, Jesus. I pray that my heart is open to receive your gifts of grace. Guide me by your Holy Spirit and strengthen my faith to follow. I pray to have complete trust in you and to use the gifts you've given to me to serve you. In the name of your beloved Son, Jesus, I pray. Amen

Questions to Consider

- What may have been the reason for God's severe test of Abraham's faith?

- How does this story of Abraham speak to the relationship he had with God?

- What relationship with God do you think the father of the boy who met Jesus may have had?

- What about this man's prayer might have appealed to Jesus?

- How does your relationship with God affect your prayers and how might your prayers affect your relationship with God?

∝FOUR℘

A Prayer for Healing

Scripture

<u>Old Testament</u>   Suggested reading: 2 Kings 20:1-11

    In those days Hezekiah became ill and was at the point of death. The prophet Isaiah son of Amoz went to him and said, "This is what the Lord says: 'Put your house in order, because you are going to die; you will not recover.' "

    Hezekiah turned his face to the wall and prayed to the Lord, "Remember, O Lord, how I have walked before you faithfully and with wholehearted devotion and have done what is good in your eyes." And Hezekiah wept bitterly.

    Before Isaiah had left the middle court, the word of the Lord came to him: "Go back and tell Hezekiah, the leader of my people, 'This is what the Lord, the God of your father David, says: I have heard your prayer and seen your tears; I will heal you. On the third day from now you will go up to the temple of the Lord. I will add fifteen years to your life. And I will deliver you and this city from the hand of the king of Assyria. I will defend this city for my sake and for the sake of my servant David.' "

    Then Isaiah said, "Prepare a poultice of figs." They did so and applied it to the boil, and he recovered. (2 Kings 20:1-7)

<u>New Testament</u>   Suggested reading: Luke 8:40-48

    As Jesus was on his way, the crowds almost crushed him. And a woman was there who had been subject to bleeding for twelve years, but no one could heal her. She came up behind him and touched the edge of his cloak, and immediately her bleeding stopped.

    "Who touched me?" Jesus asked.

When they all denied it, Peter said, "Master, the people are crowding and pressing against you."

But Jesus said, "Someone touched me; I know that power has gone out from me."

Then the woman, seeing that she could not go unnoticed, came trembling and fell at his feet. In the presence of all the people, she told why she had touched him and how she had been instantly healed. Then he said to her, "Daughter, your faith has healed you. Go in peace." (Luke: 8:42-48)

What does this Scripture mean to me?

Two simple prayers to be delivered from serious illness: One was from the Lord's faithful King Hezekiah whose first response to word of his imminent death was to turn his face to the wall and ask God to remember him; the other was from an unknown woman in the crowd who reached for the hem of Jesus' robe to be cured of a twelve-year history of bleeding. Both people were desperate, and both pleaded for healing, each in their own way. God responded to each of their appeals immediately. Why did he wait to respond to them then? Since he is omniscient, surely he knew they had been suffering.

Following a succession of kings whose weak, self-serving leadership provoked invasion by foreign powers, King Hezekiah trusted in the Lord and faithfully sought his leadership to defend the Southern Kingdom of Judah.[1] He was only a young man in his thirties when his body was overwhelmed by an infection from a boil.[2] God spoke to him through the prophet Isaiah. Responding to his brief prayer spoken in faith, God immediately directed that he be healed through the medical arts of the day—a poultice of figs applied to the lesion. His recovery enabled him to live long enough to produce an heir to the throne of David.[3]

The woman in the crowd had lived more than a decade of her life suffering with bleeding without the benefit of personal care products, sanitary bathing facilities, and front loading automatic washing machines with high efficiency detergent. After twelve years of seeking treatment from healers for continuous bleeding, she had exhausted her options. In this Jewish community, she was very likely living in isolation because she was considered "unclean" according to Hebrew law.[4]

Her social status did not deter her. Saying nothing, she simply reached out to touch Jesus' clothing and was instantly healed. Though he drew attention to her by asking who had touched him, he undoubtedly knew the answer to his own question. As she trembled in fear of retribution for having touched the teacher's robe, he responded to her tenderly referring to her as "daughter". She had established a relationship with the Son of God through the faith of her simple prayer of reaching out to him. Her willingness to admit that it was she who had touched Jesus was an articulate testimony to the crowd.

Neither of these excerpts from Scripture suggests foregoing medical treatment. God has created us with complex and wonderful bodies that are capable of healing. He has given us knowledge of nutrition, exercise, and good health habits to care for the marvelous human creatures he has created in his own image.[5] He has provided us with gifted clinicians who are educated in colleges and universities with the knowledge gained from experience and clinical research. However, even today at sophisticated medical centers equipped with the latest technology—physicians, nurses, therapists, and other medical personnel may pause to wonder when a patient, whose prognosis was grim and was expected to die, begins to improve. Others die while experiencing the best care these medical centers have to offer, though they and their loved ones may be praying for God's healing.

From my perspective today, after a career in health care, medical science still seems like the stuff of miracles. I believe it's God's response to the prayers of untold numbers of suffering people. At some point in our lives, we will encounter acute life threatening events or chronic debilitating medical conditions in ourselves or those we love. Although we may wait to pray to God when we need help, we do not live random lives.

God is sovereign in his response to our prayers. The answer to our prayers may not be what we would hope for, but we can expect the answer to be according to his plan. People we love may die even though we pray for them to live; others may live when we expect them to die. Whether we live with chronic disease or in good health, or whether the outcome of serious illness is death or life, each person's life can fulfill God's plan for the life he created.

Prayer

Our Father,

I pray for healing. (Name the person you wish to pray for and describe their disease and the suffering it is causing, remembering to include your own emotional suffering.) My heart is breaking as I think about this. I know you are all powerful to heal my loved one. I pray for your help in our lives. Use this time to strengthen my faith and my relationship with you. Help me to know your love. Help me to open my heart to your grace and accept your will for our lives. I pray through Jesus, your Son, my Lord. Amen

Questions to Consider

- Like Hezekiah, when you're facing a crisis in your life, is your first response to reach out to God in faith?

- God spoke to Hezekiah through his prophet, Isaiah. Has he spoken to you through someone in your life?

- After twelve years of suffering and unsuccessful treatment, why do you think the woman with bleeding was healed instantly?

- How could God use illness to strengthen our relationship with him?

- Can we trust God completely with our lives?

ℭℨFIVE℘

A Prayer in Time of Grief

Scripture

<u>Old Testament</u>   Suggested reading: Genesis 6:5-22; 7; 8; 9:1-17

    The Lord saw how great man's wickedness on earth had become, and that every inclination of the thoughts of his heart was only evil all the time. The Lord was grieved that he had made man on earth, and his heart was filled with pain. (Genesis: 6:5, 6)

<u>New Testament</u>   Suggested reading: John 11:1-44

    Jesus wept. (John 11:35)

What does this Scripture mean to me?

From the story of creation recorded in the book of Genesis, we learn that we were created in the image of God.[1] We may be amazed to think of God experiencing the emotions of grief and pain! These are emotions many may ascribe solely to the condition of being human. While we may not be certain of precisely what is implicit to be created in the image of God, I believe he has given us emotions like those he himself experiences. Throughout Scripture, we read of God characterized by other emotions such as love, anger, and compassion.

    As God was establishing his kingdom on earth, he sometimes took action that seems astonishing. The story of Noah building and inhabiting the ark with his family and the animals of God's creation is one of those times. In this story, we learn that he obliterated life on earth with a flood. The earth was so full of violence, and the people had become so corrupt that he was sorry (i.e., "grieved") that he had created them.

He found favor with Noah because "...he was a righteous man...and walked with God".[2] The story of Noah building the ark for his family and two of every kind of animal, male and female, was a favorite of mine as a young child who learned of the story in Sunday school. The climax of the story is God's covenant with Noah, his descendants, and all life on earth for all generations to come. He promised never again to flood the entire earth to destroy all life. The rainbow was to be a sign to remind us of this covenant. Given the sheer beauty and drama of a rainbow, after his grieving, we can see God's joy in this promise he surely wants us to remember!

We glimpse God's grief again when Jesus shed tears following the death of his friend Lazarus. It seems puzzling that Jesus was suddenly sad because, as God, he is omniscient and, therefore, must have known that Lazarus was sick and would die. He traveled to the home of Lazarus in Bethany even though his disciples reminded him that the Jews had tried to stone him there on an earlier occasion. This trip was important enough to defy danger.

Jesus encountered a scene of mourning at the home of Lazarus' sisters, Martha and Mary. When he saw his friend Mary weeping, "...he was deeply moved in spirit and troubled."[3] Jesus had heartfelt compassion for her suffering in grief for the loss of her brother. He undoubtedly knew he would raise Lazarus from death to life again, yet he wept in empathy for his friends.

I believe he grieves with us when we experience loss in our own lives. We know that life on earth inevitably brings with it loss and sorrow. But, we are assured that God knows our pain and wants us to open our hearts to his healing hope.

God has given us a new covenant. Jesus reassured Lazarus' sister, Martha, with these words:

> *"I am the resurrection and the life. He who believes in me will live, even though he dies; and whoever lives and believes in me will never die."* (John 11:25)

During times of deep grief, it's difficult and may even feel impossible to be hopeful about the future. Even in the depth of our grief for the most significant losses we experience, Jesus' promise can give us hope. The Holy Spirit whispers to our heart to let Jesus grieve with us.[4] There may be no time more important than this to listen to God speak to our heart.

Prayer

Lord Jesus,

In my grief, I can hardly speak. My pain is so overwhelming, it clouds my thoughts. (Try to tell Jesus about the pain you feel for the loss of your loved one.) I have cried until it feels as if I have no more tears to weep. Help me endure this excruciating pain. Please relieve me of the agonizing anxiety that I have done something to deserve this. I know you are present with me. I trust you to understand my suffering. In my suffering, forgive me for my loss of hope. I fall silent to hear your Spirit speak of hope to my heart. In your name I pray. Amen

Questions to Consider

- Have you thought before of God experiencing the pain of grief?

- How do you think God, the Father, felt when his Son, Jesus, was tortured and dying on the cross?

- If God knows everything, why does he want you to pray when he knows you're feeling miserable?

- Do you think Jesus can really empathize with your pain?

- Have you ever thought of God really feeling the emotion of love for you?

ᏗSIXᏜ

A Prayer for Help with Anxiety

Scripture

<u>Old Testament</u>   Suggested reading: 1Kings 3:4-28;
                      Ecclesiastes 1:1-14; 3:1-14; 5:8-15; 12:9-14

What has been will be again,
    what has been done will be done again;
    there is nothing new under the sun.
There is a time for everything,
and a season for every activity under heaven:
a time to be born and a time to die,
a time to plant and a time to uproot,
a time to kill and a time to heal,
a time to tear down and a time to build,
a time to weep and a time to laugh,
a time to mourn and a time to dance.
Naked a man comes from his mother's womb,
    and as he comes, so he departs.
    ...here is the conclusion of the matter:
Fear God and keep his commandments,
    for this is the whole duty of man.
    (Ecclesiastes 1:9; 3:1-4; 5:15; 12:13)

<u>New Testament</u>   Suggested reading: Mathew 6:19-34

    "Look at the birds of the air; they do not sow or reap or store away in barns, and yet your heavenly Father feeds them. Are you not much more valuable than they? Who of you by worrying can add a single hour to his life?"

"And why do you worry about clothes? See how the lilies of the field grow. They do not labor or spin. Yet I tell you that not even Solomon in all his splendor was dressed like one of these. If that is how God clothes the grass of the field, which is here today and tomorrow is thrown in the fire, will he not much more clothe you, O you of little faith? So do not worry, saying, 'What shall we eat?' or 'What shall we drink?' or 'What shall we wear?' For the pagans run after all these things, and your heavenly Father knows that you need them. But seek first his kingdom and his righteousness, and all these things will be given to you as well. Therefore do not worry about tomorrow, for tomorrow will worry about itself." (Mathew 6:26-34)

What does this Scripture mean to me?

King Solomon, the favored son of King David, was anointed to succeed his father as the King of Israel. He was a young man when he ascended the throne and, because of his youth, he was inexperienced as a leader. Through a dream, God promised him the gift of a "discerning heart" which was the source of the wisdom for which he became known.[1] King Solomon is thought by many to be the author of Ecclesiastes, though it would seem to have been later in his reign.[2] Solomon made observations about life that are consistent with those spoken by Jesus almost a 1,000 years later.

An initial reading of Ecclesiastes may leave the reader feeling as though the author was fatalistic: We can't predict the future and good and bad happen to both the righteous and the wicked. As the author repeats, it seems "meaningless".[3] Solomon was able to discern that God was the sovereign ruler of the cycle of life. The pattern of life—that we are born, we live, and we die—is brief and similar for all of us regardless of our beliefs or our perceived social status.

Despite the organized lives we live in our civilized society, we allow our lives to be consumed with stress and anxiety. We may work hard, build our resumes, and negotiate higher salaries or find ourselves working on an assembly line waiting for the next layoff. Or, we may be struggling to find work to support a family at a basic level of subsistence in a complex economic system in which we find ourselves near the bottom. In any case, we may be reluctant to seek God first and put our trust in him to provide for us and our families. King Solomon observed that the only significant difference in our lives is the condition of fearing God.

We could make similar observations in our own lifetime. A major premise of science, that we learn in school as children, is that we can neither create nor destroy matter.[4] We can rearrange the molecules of matter but the basic elements remain. We can discover new substances from matter that was previously created, and we can combine them to invent new uses. Initially, some may seem life altering, like new communication technology, only to see it become outdated by a newer version or even disintegrate. For example, with an earthquake followed by a tsunami as occurred in Japan in 2011, the people living in an epicenter of technological advancement were reduced to communicating with lost loved ones through messages scrawled on the walls of evacuation centers or with scraps of paper taped to message boards.[5] Millennia ago, King Solomon identified that "…there is nothing new under the sun." God is the ruler and King of his creation.

Jesus' words from the Sermon on the Mount, which we read in this passage from the Gospel of Mathew, speak to us about this understanding that God is in charge. God has ordered his creation with a time for everything. The voice of Jesus is clear, "Do not worry about tomorrow, for tomorrow will worry about itself."[6] Perhaps Jesus used metaphors from nature to help us understand our place in the order of God's creation. Instead of wasting our time and thought with worry, he tells us to seek God first and he will take even better care of us than he cares for the birds and lilies of the field. As we read the words spoken by Jesus, the words of King Solomon seem to echo that the whole duty of each of us is to seek God first. Nothing is more important than having a relationship with God, trusting that he will provide for us if we place our trust in him.

Jesus doesn't suggest to us that we should lead a lazy life of idleness but that we avoid wasting our talents and energy distracted with anxiety. I believe God gives us the opportunity to communicate with him through prayer to enable us to trust him to provide us with the resources and protection we need. He invites us to find rest in his embrace as we trust that he will provide for us.

Prayer

Heavenly Father,

Forgive me for letting my mind fill with anxiety about my material and emotional needs. (Think about the things that you are anxious about and identify them as you talk with God.) I pray that you will give me strength of faith to trust you completely with my life. Help me trust you with the lives of those I love. Keep me aware that they are not my possessions, but your children, and that each of us has a separate relationship with you. Help me remember that you will care for each of them apart from me. Through your Son, Jesus, I pray. Amen

Questions to Consider

- What does Solomon identify as the only discernable difference in the life of each person?

- What are your thoughts about giving God complete trust in your life?

- What, specifically, do you have concern about when you think about giving God complete control for the direction of your life?

- Why might anxiety be something that reflects lack of trust in God?

- How could you apply this to your prayers to God about your worries?

⋘SEVEN⋙

A Prayer for Forgiveness

Scripture

<u>Old Testament</u>   Suggested reading: 2 Samuel 11; 12:1-24; Psalm 51

Have mercy on me, O God, according to your unfailing love;
    according to your great compassion blot out my
    transgressions.
Create in me a clean heart, O God,
    and renew a steadfast spirit within me.
Do not cast me from your presence
    or take your Holy Spirit from me.
Restore to me the joy of your salvation
    and grant me a willing spirit, to sustain me. (Psalm 51:1, 10-12)

<u>New Testament</u>   Suggested reading: Luke 15:11-31

"So he got up and went to his father.

But while he was still a long way off, his father saw him and was filled with compassion for him; he ran to his son, threw his arms around him and kissed him.

The son said to him, 'Father, I have sinned against heaven and against you. I am no longer worthy to be called your son.'

But the father said to his servants, 'Quick! Bring the best robe and put it on him. Put a ring on his finger and sandals on his feet. Bring the fattened calf and kill it. Let's have a feast and celebrate. For this son of mine was dead and is alive again; he was lost and is found.' " (Luke 15:20-24)

What does this Scripture mean to me?

In 2 Samuel, chapters eleven and twelve, we learn that David, the second man anointed as king of Israel, was smitten by the beauty of Bathsheba. She was married to Uriah, a young officer in Israel's army. While Uriah was away at war, from the rooftop of the palace, King David observed Bathsheba bathing in a nearby courtyard. He summoned her to join him at the palace and took her to his bed chamber. Some weeks later, she learned she was pregnant.

David was a shrewd man and devised a deception to cover up his responsibility for the outcome of this adulterous affair. He sent word to Joab, his commander in the field, to order Uriah to return to Jerusalem on the pretense of receiving a report on the progress of the troops. When Uriah returned to Jerusalem, David offered him a night of rest at home with his wife, Bathsheba, but Uriah declined. Out of loyalty to the servants who accompanied him, Uriah spent the night sleeping on mats outside with his servants. Not to be deterred, the next day David invited Uriah to dine with him at the palace and offered him plenty of wine, hoping he would get drunk, dulling his judgment and his resolve to stay with his servants. Still, he did not go home to sleep with Bathsheba. David's scheme to cover his tracks was foiled by another man's righteousness!

When he sent Uriah back to the field of battle, he sent a note with him for Joab, his commander. The note instructed Joab to put Uriah on the front line where it was most likely that he would die in battle. As planned, Uriah was killed. After Bathsheba's period of mourning, David was free to marry her. However, God's anointed king was forced to face the consequences of his adultery with Bathsheba and the ruthless murder of her husband, Uriah. He was visited by the prophet, Nathan, who convicted him of his sin at the root of this tragedy. David's joy with his new marriage was short-lived when the child conceived with Bathsheba died a week after his birth—only the beginning of the family calamities he would endure.

Realizing he had not only sinned against Uriah but against God, King David must have been overwhelmed by the guilt weighing heavily on his heart. He was keenly aware that his leadership of Israel would be effective only through the sovereign will of God and through his guidance.[1] Whatever the depravity of his sin, he truly trusted God not to abandon him. His passionate prayer, pleading with God for forgiveness, is recorded in Psalm 51.[2]

Jesus provided another model for forgiveness in the parable of the prodigal son found in Luke's Gospel. He told the story of a man who had two sons. The younger son was impetuous and asked his father for his share of the estate before his father had died. The father complied with this request and divided the estate between his two sons. The younger son left for distant places where he squandered his fortune with a wild lifestyle while the elder son stayed home to manage his father's property. After dissipating his fortune, the younger son found work feeding pigs but, during this time of famine, he was starving. This crisis in his life brought him insight into the huge mistake he had made and the consequences he was suffering. He decided to go home to plead with his father for forgiveness. He would admit that he wasn't worthy of being his son and ask his father for a job so he would at least have food and shelter.

The father ran out to meet his rebellious son with unconditional joy that his son had returned home! He threw his arms around him and kissed him.[3] As the son pleaded for forgiveness, the father asked the servants to bring the best robe, a ring, and sandals for the feet of his wayward son. He instructed them to prepare a fattened calf for a celebration in his honor.

Later in this chapter of Luke, we read that the compliant elder son angrily confronted his father complaining about the generous forgiveness his father had offered to his brother. His complaint was based on his own willingness to stay home and obediently work the estate while his brother ran off and wasted his share. The father forgave the behavior of both sons, and he reminded the jealous elder son that he had always had the advantages of living on his father's estate. He invited him to share in his joy and to join the party to celebrate the return of his lost brother.

Our Father still runs out to meet us. He still wraps his arms around us. He still loves us. He still forgives us for all of our sins—for stubbornly refusing to live with him, for squandering his love, and for envying his loving relationship with others. We have only to return and admit that, on our own, we're not worthy of his grace. We can trust that the sacrifice of his Son, Jesus, will cover our sins.

Prayer

Lord God, my Father,

I come to you with a heavy heart, burdened with the guilt of my sin. I know I can't hide from you. You know the secrets of my heart, even those I try to hide from myself. I plead with you to forgive the sins that are weighing on me and cleanse my heart. (Take time to think about these sins and name them to yourself and to God.) Forgive me for squandering the gifts you have given to me, and forgive the petty envy I have for your generosity and love for other people. I pray that you will renew my faith in your Holy Spirit to help me live my life trusting in your guidance to live the life you have planned for me. Through your Son, Jesus Christ, I pray for forgiveness and your peace in my heart. Amen

Questions to Consider

- How could God have loved King David, a man who was capable of murder and adultery?

- How did David's sin affect his relationship with God?

- Do you think there are consequences for sin today?

- Could God use a crisis in your life to speak to you?

- Have you experienced a crisis in your life that has brought you insight about living the life God has planned for you?

⋆EIGHT⋆

A Prayer of Joy

Scripture

<u>Old Testament</u>   Suggested reading: 1 Samuel 1; 2:1-11

Then Hannah prayed and said:
"My heart rejoices in the Lord;
  in the Lord my horn is lifted high.
My mouth boasts over my enemies,
  for I delight in your deliverance.
There is no one holy like the Lord;
  there is no one besides you;
  there is no Rock like our God." (1 Samuel 2:1-3)

<u>New Testament</u>   Suggested reading: Luke 1:26-56

And Mary said:
"My soul glorifies the Lord
  and my spirit rejoices in God my Savior,
for he has been mindful
  of the humble state of his servant.
From now on all generations will call me blessed,
  for the Mighty One has done great things for me—
  holy is his name.
He has helped his servant Israel
  remembering to be merciful
to Abraham and his descendants forever,
  even as he said to our fathers." (Luke 1:46-50, 54, 55)

What does this Scripture mean to me?

These are excerpts from the prayers of two women whose hearts rejoice that God has created life within them. Mary's prayer may be the better known as the Magnificat, but Hannah's Song is thought by many to be a Scripture source on which the Magnificat of Mary was closely patterned.[1] The joy of these young women was deeply felt. As Mary anticipates bearing the Son of God, she describes joy that "glorifies" her soul. In our experience, we may know the joy of the long awaited birth of a child in our own family or in the family of a beloved friend. God blesses us with the creation of life.

Hannah suffered great humiliation as the barren wife of a man who loved her but who was also married to another woman who had borne him several children. In ancient biblical times, infertility was disgraceful because it was thought to be a sign of disfavor with God. Year after year, Hannah was tormented by her inability to bear a child. Finally, as she wept in prayer, she vowed to God that, if he would grant her a child, she would dedicate the child to God's service. Hannah conceived and did as she promised. When her son, Samuel, was still a very young child, she took him to live at the temple with Eli, the high priest. He grew to be a leader of the Israelites as the last judge of Israel and God's faithful prophet who God called to anoint the first kings of Israel.[2, 3]

How could Hannah give up her child for this purpose? Hannah had made a vow to God and trusted God to care for the son that he created in response to her prayer. She realized that Samuel was not her possession, just as all children are God's creation; though they are a blessing to their parents, they belong to God.[4] Hannah's prayer of joy reflected her relationship with God. She understood that God is omniscient and knew the longings and hidden secrets of her heart. She also understood that he is the sovereign creator of life. He was fulfilling his plan for her life and his kingdom.

Mary, a young woman in her teens, had only recently learned from an angel that she was to bear the Messiah, the Son of God. Although it was not unusual for girls of her age to marry, since she was a virgin and betrothed but unmarried, she knew she would be ridiculed and disgraced in her community if she was outspoken about her pregnancy.[5] Who could she trust to understand what was happening to her? God provided an answer through an angel who told her that her relative, Elizabeth, who had been barren, had been pregnant for six months. Mary hurried to see Elizabeth. As Mary was arriving at her home and Elizabeth heard her voice, the child in her womb (who later grew to be known as John the Baptist) leaped as Elizabeth was filled with the Holy Spirit. She understood Mary's situation without an explanation and exclaimed, "Blessed are you among women, and blessed is the child you will bear!"[6]

Mary's response was the prayer well known as the Magnificat. Like Hannah, she obeyed God as his humble servant. She realized that he had chosen her to bear his Son, the Messiah, to fulfill his promise to Israel. Like Hannah, Mary was confident in her relationship with God. Both Hannah and Mary were real people. Although perhaps the more beautiful words of their prayers are quoted here, each of them had an honest relationship with God and expressed some thoughts in their prayers that, today, may even be described as vindictive. They relied on God to protect them and prayed to God in words that came naturally to them—just as God wants us to speak with him. He knows our hearts. We can't keep anything secret from him.

To the cynics who would dismiss the response of God to Hannah's prayer or the conception of a child to the virgin, Mary, as Jewish or Christian myths about supernatural events, one might ask, "What good is a God who is not omnipotent?" Scripture is filled with miracles attesting to the power of God. We can trust that he is still that powerful today.

Prayer

Lord God, my Father,

My heart is filled with joy for your love for me and the precious children you have sent into my life. (Name the children who are precious to you whether or not they are in your family.) Help me always to remember that they are your children and not my possessions. Show me the way to support your plan for their lives. I trust that they are in your care and that you are with them as you are with me. Keep me mindful that you love them even more than I do. Help me to trust confidently in your love. Through your Son, Jesus Christ, I pray. Amen

Questions to Consider

- How could Hannah have dedicated Samuel to the Lord when he was at such a young age?

- What might have been Mary's thoughts when she was informed by an angel that she would be the mother of the Messiah?

- What are your thoughts about the miracle of Jesus' conception?

- Have you experienced miracles that you have thought of as "coincidences" in your own life?

- When you give it serious thought, do you believe that God has been speaking to your heart?

ଔNINEৡ

A Prayer for a Generous Heart

Scripture

<u>Old Testament</u>   Suggested reading: Proverbs 14:20-31; 29:6-14

> He who oppresses the poor shows contempt for their Maker,
>   but whoever is kind to the needy honors God.
> The righteous care about justice for the poor,
>   but the wicked have no such concern.
> The poor man and the oppressor have this in common:
>   The Lord gives sight to the eyes of both.
> (Proverbs 14:31; 29:7, 13)

<u>New Testament</u>   Suggested reading: Mathew 25:31-46

"Then the King will say to those on his right, 'Come, you who are blessed by my Father; take your inheritance, the kingdom prepared for you since the creation of the world. For I was hungry and you gave me something to eat, I was thirsty and you gave me something to drink, I was a stranger and you invited me in. I needed clothes and you clothed me, I was sick and you looked after me, I was in prison and you came to visit me.'

Then the righteous will answer him, 'Lord, when did we see you hungry and feed you, or thirsty and give you something to drink? When did we see you a stranger and invite you in, or needing clothes and clothe you? When did we see you sick or in prison and go to visit you?"

The King will reply, 'I tell you the truth, whatever you did for one of the least of these brothers of mine, you did for me.' "
(Mathew 25:34-40)

What does this Scripture mean to me?

Since ancient biblical times, God's people have had the responsibility of serving God by providing for those who lack the essentials for living such as food, clothing, and shelter. King Solomon, the author of this wisdom literature from the book of Proverbs, describes our responsibilities to those who are poor with words like "kind", "concern", "justice". These words imply that our responsibilities go beyond financial help to advocacy and offers of human kindness. We are told that in sharing our blessings, we honor God but when we show distain for those with less, we show contempt for God. God expects more than kind thoughts but action; he expects more than action but genuine feelings of kindness. He expects us not only to give but to love giving.

Jesus' words from the New Testament seldom fail to bring tears to my eyes as I think of all my lost opportunities to care for the suffering poor, to give voice to those who have no power to be heard, to grab my courage in my hands and touch the lives of those who are sick, and even to reach out to people in prison or ex-offenders who need a new start in life. And more, Jesus wants me to do it for them as if I were doing it for him. From the beginning of my life, God has given me everything I have that is good. Nothing I have *belongs* to me. What thin line separates me from those who need my help?

Have you ever found yourself turning your head to avoid looking into the eyes of someone who seems *needy*? Or, brushed past a Salvation Army bell ringer to avoid really seeing that person when you don't have any intention of contributing? I have. When I've done that, I found myself feeling as though I had avoided the eyes of Jesus.

If we think about this rationally, there are too many reasons to avoid doing what God expects. We have significant financial responsibilities for ourselves and our own family and, no matter how our income might expand or contract, we always seem to need more income to support our obligations. As we think about those who are poor, we question what responsibility they have to dig themselves out of the hole they are in and wonder why they didn't plan for a better future supported by the wise decisions, hard work, and education necessary to achieve it. Even if we can concede that there are some people who are the innocent victims of poverty or disaster, how do we know that any money we might contribute will get to the people who really need it? How do we know that we're not just wasting our precious time to help people who will accept our help but will never learn to help themselves?

The bottom-line is that these questions are based on the source of the rationale that keeps us from following God's expectations. Everything we have that is good is from God including the gifts of energy, motivation, talent, and creativity. Jesus tells us that we can expect the poor to be with us.[1] As we read this Scripture, it seems clear that he wants us to care for them as if we were caring for him.

While it's a fact that some organizations asking for donations are corrupt, contemporary ratings which identify charitable organizations that are trustworthy are as available as the internet.[2] Although some people we try to help seem destined to live a life of poverty and deprivation, worthy organizations in our own communities earnestly appeal to us to use our God-given talents to help those in need. Many, who just need a "hand up" to live productive lives, will be capable of helping others!

For me, this isn't about what is rational. It's about the condition of my heart. Left on my own, my heart is as hard as a rock, and my eyes avert the gaze of Jesus looking at me through the eyes of someone who needs my help. Skeptics might ask, if there is a God, does he care for those who are poor, sick, or victimized? It's only at the foot of the cross that I can kneel in prayer and find relief for my stingy heart. I appeal to Jesus to help me to give and to love giving, to share and to love sharing, to learn to love the people he puts in my pathway to provide his help with my hands, my time, the talent, and the financial resources he has given to me. Out of gratitude for his generous love, how can I refuse?

Prayer

Lord Jesus,

You know my heart. You know that without your help, my heart is as cold as stone. I am miserly and find many reasons to hoard the gifts you have given to me. (Think of times when you have found excuses for not sharing God's blessings to you.) Help me confront the truth and forgive me for the secret distain I have for those who are less prosperous than I. Help me open my heart to you. Soften it with your love to enable me to be generous—to give and to love giving. Amen

Questions to Consider

- What does generosity have to do with our relationship with God?

- Why do you think that God depends on us to provide for those who need help?

- How do you feel about people who have less than you?

- Can you think of times that you have avoided sharing your gifts?

- What can you ask God do about the condition of your heart?

☙TEN❧

A Prayer of Thanks

Scripture

Old Testament   Suggested reading: 1 Chronicles 15; 16:1-36

Give thanks to the Lord, call on his name;
>make known among the nations what he has done.
Sing to him, sing praise to him;
>tell of all his wonderful acts.
Glory in his holy name;
>let the hearts of those who seek the Lord rejoice.
Look to the Lord and his strength;
>seek his face always.
Bring an offering and come before him;
>worship the Lord in the splendor of his holiness.
Tremble before him, all the earth!
>The world is firmly established; it cannot be moved.
Let the heavens rejoice, let the earth be glad;
>let them say among the nations, "The Lord reigns!"
>(1Chronicles 16:8-11, 29-31)

New Testament   Suggested reading: Philippians 1:1-9

I thank my God every time I remember you. In all my prayers
for all of you, I always pray with joy because of your partnership in
the gospel from the first day until now, being confident of this, that
he who began a good work in you will carry it on to completion until
the day of Christ Jesus. (Philippians 1:3-6)

What does this Scripture mean to me?

The ark of the covenant was a chest crafted and carved for the interior chamber of the tabernacle as God directed Moses while the Israelites were wandering in the dessert.[1] Among its contents were the stone tablets on which the Ten Commandments were written.[2] The ark was a precious reminder to the Israelites that God was present with them. It was so important to their trust in God that there were very specific rules for its care, including exactly by whom and how it could be transported from one location to another.[3]

Decades before King David uttered this eloquent prayer, the Israelites were misguided about the significance of the ark and attempted to use it to ensure success in battle with the Philistines.[4] The Philistines were impressed with God's protection of Israel and assumed they could capture the God of the Israelites by capturing the ark. After capturing it, as the Philistines moved the location of the ark, they believed misfortune, caused by Israel's God, followed it. Perplexed, they decided to return it to the Israelites.[5]

Israel's first king, Saul, seemed to ignore the significance of the ark. Not so, King David, the warrior-king and champion of Israel. After defeating the Philistine army, he made arrangements to transport the ark to a more secure location. The transportation was done with some bravado—without careful attention to following the required rules for transport and care of the ark. When a man died as a result, God was able to use this event to help David understand that he expected unconditional obedience.[6]

Imagine David's great relief and gratitude to God after Israel defeated the Philistines, and the ark was successfully relocated to a tent he had specifically fabricated and erected for it. King David's prayer reflects the faith of a man who is grateful for his relationship with God. He had demonstrated that he would trust God completely to lead him as God's servant-king.

Like David, the apostle Paul gave thanks for relationship with God. His prayer of thanks was for the Philippians and their support of his ministry among them. The man perhaps best known as Christianity's first missionary, Paul was originally named Saul. He comes to our attention as we read about the stoning of Stephen, one of the seven men chosen by the early Christian community to help spread the word of Christ.[7] Saul believed he was following God's law when he became legendary for persecuting Christians. The powerful story of his conversion is recorded in the book of Acts.[8]

After his conversion, the apostle Paul was called to be a missionary to preach the Gospel to both Jews and Gentiles. He traveled by ship to cities on the shores of the Mediterranean Sea as well as to lands surrounding the coast, to Asia Minor and Macedonia, where he established a church in the city of Philippi, a Roman Colony.[9] Although he had previously suffered indignities and torture, Paul, a Roman citizen, was protected from death but imprisoned on a type of house arrest when wrote this letter to the Philippians.[10]

Paul was zealous in his missionary work and devoted to those to whom he preached but, like King David, he respected the will of God. It was this relationship with Christ that the apostle Paul shared with the church at Philippi for which he gave thanks in this letter. Although he was grateful for his partnership in Christ with the Philippians, he understood that his work was to obediently bring God's message of salvation to both the Jews and the Gentiles according to God's own plan—just as God continued the dynasty of King David according to his own plan.[11] Paul authored much of the New Testament and, as he waited for his trial in Rome for two years, he continued to write and teach about Jesus Christ.[12]

Prayer

Lord God,

Thank you for your willingness to have a relationship with me even when I'm disobedient. (Identify the times when you know you have recently been disobedient to God's will for your life.) I pray for your forgiveness for my disobedience. Please forgive me for proceeding to disobey you even when I knew what I was doing was wrong. Thank you for loving me. I pray for strength of faith to follow the guidance of your Holy Spirit to obediently live the life you have given to me. In Jesus' name I pray. Amen

Questions to Consider

- What do you think King David learned from his first attempt to transport the ark of the covenant?

- Why might obedience have been so important to David's relationship with God?

- What do the expressions of thanks of King David and the apostle Paul have in common?

- How could Paul's background as both a Jew and a Roman citizen have been important to his work as a missionary?

- How might your background be important in God's plan for your life?

⋆ELEVEN⋆

A Prayer for Humility

Scripture

<u>Old Testament</u>   Suggested reading: Isaiah 42:1-9

"Here is my servant, whom I uphold,
    my chosen one in whom I delight;
I will put my Spirit on him
    and he will bring justice to the nations.
I, the Lord, have called you in righteousness;
    I will hold your hand.
I will keep you and will make you
    to be a covenant for the people,
    and a light for the Gentiles." (Isaiah 42:1, 6)

<u>New Testament</u>   Suggested reading: John 13:1-17

Jesus knew that the Father had put all things under his power, and that he had come from God and was returning to God; so he got up from the meal, took off his outer clothing, and wrapped a towel around his waist. After that, he poured water into a basin and began to wash his disciples' feet, drying them with the towel that was wrapped around him.

When he had finished washing their feet, he put on his clothes and returned to his place. "Do you understand what I have done for you?" he asked them. "You call me 'Teacher' and 'Lord', and rightly so, for that is what I am. Now that I, your Lord and Teacher, have washed your feet, you also should wash one another's feet. I have set you an example that you should do as I have done for you. I tell you the truth, no servant is greater than his master, nor is a messenger greater than the one who sent him. Now that you know these things, you will be blessed if you do them." (John 13:3-5, 12-17)

What does this Scripture mean to me?

Isaiah, God's great prophet of judgment and hope, revealed what God had spoken to him through visions.[1] He warned the people of the Southern Kingdom, Judah, that their rebellion against God would lead to condemnation through foreign invasion. He used this song of poetry to capture the attention of the people as he described God's compassion for them. Even though they had forsaken him and would be captured and forced into exile, God had plans to fulfill the covenant he had made with his people while his servant, David, was King of Israel.

Isaiah, through his poetry, brought word from God that his "servant", the Messiah, would be a "light" to the Gentiles and that he would establish a new covenant for all people. More than 600 years before the birth of Jesus, Isaiah envisioned God's plan to continue his kingdom as the sovereign king over the world he had created. So powerful is our God that he confidently sent his Son as his servant, a baby who would mature to serve as a humble itinerant preacher before being crucified as a criminal, to redeem his people and bring justice to all nations. Although the people Jesus called to be his original twelve disciples were flawed and ordinary young Jewish men, he chose them to initiate the transformation of the world through the new covenant he established. Jesus was the Messiah, the servant, as Isaiah had prophesied.

The night of his arrest, while his last evening meal with his disciples was being served, Jesus gave his disciples an eloquent lesson in humility. After days of traveling on foot through pastures and fields or on dusty roads littered with animal droppings, their feet were likely to be filthy. It was the duty of the household servants to bring a basin of water to wash the feet of the guests as they reclined at the table for the meal. (So important had washing of feet as a sign of service become that the apostle Paul later used it as an example to identify those who lived lives of service pleasing to God.)[2]

For me, this simple act of Jesus, serving his disciples by washing their feet, is a powerful metaphor to convey a message of humbling one's heart to serve others. It was a striking demonstration to help us understand that, as his disciples, what is important is the message our behavior conveys about Jesus Christ. Not only is my arrogance a wall that I use in a vain attempt to shield myself from God's omniscience and his expectations for my life, but it could be a stumbling block to those who would open their hearts to God if not for the condescension I convey with my false pride.[3]

His willingness, to accept the role of servant and wash the feet of his disciples, reminds me that my life has no meaning if not for Jesus' willingness to humble himself to offer me redemption by washing me to cleanse me of my sin. It reminds me that my life is blessed when my heart opens to the truth that I am no better than anyone else, that I have no special entitlement. God loves me, and he loves my brothers and sisters throughout the world. He expects me to wash their feet—to serve them as he has served those who follow him.

Prayer

Lord Jesus,

Thank you for humbling yourself to redeem me. When I think about your example of humility, my heart hurts with the memory of times I have arrogantly thought of my brothers and sisters with distain—as though I am more important or precious to you than they are. (Think about the times you have thought about others with distain.) I pray that you will forgive me for my pride and I ask that you will help me know the ways that I can wash the feet of your people. Help my heart know the honor of serving you by serving others. In your name I pray. Amen

Questions to Consider

- Why do you think it was God's plan to send his Son to the world as a servant?

- How could Jesus confidently entrust such ordinary young men to begin the transformation of the world with God's new covenant?

- What is so important about the lesson of humble service that Jesus used the last hours before his arrest and crucifixion to teach this to his disciples?

- How has your arrogance kept you from accepting the humility of Jesus?

- Has God spoken to your heart about opportunities for washing the feet of others?

☙TWELVE❧

A Prayer when Feeling Betrayed

Scripture

<u>Old Testament</u>   Suggested reading: Genesis 37:1-36; 39; 40; 41; 42; 43; 44; 45

Then Joseph said to his brothers, "Come close to me." When they had done so, he said, "I am your brother, Joseph, the one you sold into Egypt! And now, do not be distressed and do not be angry with yourselves for selling me here, because it was to save lives that God sent me ahead of you. For two years now there has been famine in the land, and for the next five years there will not be plowing and reaping. But God sent me ahead of you to preserve for you a remnant on earth and to save your lives by a great deliverance." (Genesis 45:4-7)

<u>New Testament</u>   Suggested reading: Mathew 26:17-50; 27:1-10

When evening came, Jesus was reclining at the table with the Twelve. And while they were eating, he said, "I tell you the truth, one of you will betray me."

They were very sad and began to say to him one after the other, "Surely not I, Lord?"

Jesus replied, "The one who has dipped his hand into the bowl with me will betray me. The Son of Man will go just as it is written about him. But woe to that man who betrays the Son of Man! It would be better for him if he had not been born."

Then Judas, the one who would betray him said, "Surely not I, Rabbi?"

Jesus answered, "Yes, it is you." (Mathew 26:20-25)

What does this Scripture mean to me?

Betrayal—disloyalty so crushing it has potential to threaten the life of its quarry and ambushes a relationship based on an expectation of faithfulness. Should husbands and wives expect infidelity in marriage? Should children expect their parents to neglect or abuse them? Should brothers expect their siblings to sell them as slaves? Questions like these may help us give voice to the betrayal we experience in our own lives. Since ancient times, society has adopted boundaries that allow us to live life with certain expectations. When these are breached, the impact can be devastating. How do we move beyond the excruciating pain of betrayal? The well known story of Joseph, from the book of Genesis, describes a rare outcome of harsh family betrayal.

Joseph, the son of Jacob and his favorite wife Rachel, was his father's favorite son. Like many families of that day and time, due to polygamy, children lived with siblings who were born to different mothers. Perhaps the family circumstances these children experienced were somewhat like the children of contemporary blended families pieced together following divorce and remarriage. Jacob was unabashed in his favoritism of Joseph and lavished him with a robe to wear that was much finer than any he provided to his ten older sons. Naturally, Joseph's brothers were jealous. Any parent today might wonder why Joseph's father would set him up so brazenly. As if his relationship with his brothers was not already strained, Joseph revealed his dreams in which the obvious interpretation was that one day his brothers would bow down honoring him. Looking through the lens of dysfunctional families which thrive as commonly in the 21st century as they did in ancient times, we might expect negative family dynamics to emerge with calamitous results.

To make matters worse, one day Jacob unwittingly sent his precious son, Joseph, to check on his brothers who were tending the family flocks in pastures that were remote from the family compound. As they saw him coming, his brothers plotted to kill their brother, "...that dreamer".[1] It was only through the shrewd maneuvering of his oldest brother, Rueben, that his life was spared. Rueben persuaded his bothers to tie Joseph up and throw him into an empty cistern. Later that day, they sold him for twenty shekels of silver to a caravan of traders traveling to Egypt.

Purchased to be a servant of the captain of the guard, Joseph was later imprisoned on false accusations of seducing the captain's wife. The prison warden valued Joseph's capabilities and gave him responsibility to manage the prison inmates. One of these inmates was the former cupbearer to the pharaoh. Although Joseph correctly interpreted this inmate's dream that he would be reinstated to his position at court, the cupbearer failed to mention this to the pharaoh until two years later when the pharaoh himself was struggling with the meaning of his own dreams. When other officials failed to be able to interpret his dreams, based on the cupbearer's self-serving report of his past experience, the pharaoh summoned Joseph from prison. Joseph's God-given gift of dream interpretation enabled him to advise the pharaoh about the meaning of his dream: It was a prediction of a prosperous seven-year harvest followed by seven years of famine.

As a result of the pharaoh's confidence in Joseph, he was appointed to a position of prominence perhaps similar to a combination of what we know as the Secretaries of Agriculture, Commerce, and the Interior, though likely even more important in this ancient agrarian-based economy. It was the famine which propelled Joseph's bothers to evoke the dream of Joseph's youth. Jacob, unaware of Joseph's position or even that he was still alive, sent his sons to Egypt to secure food. When his brothers encountered him, rather than rejecting them, Joseph embraced them. He now understood that his betrayal by his brothers was part of God's plan for the purpose of his life to preserve the remnant of God's kingdom on earth.

Unlike Joseph, Jesus was entirely aware of his Father's purpose for his life. The omniscient Son of God, he expected Judas to betray him. His sobering response to Judas, at this last evening meal with his disciples, contrasts with the poignant embrace of Joseph and his brothers. Judas was confronting God himself whom he would betray with a kiss for which he had negotiated payment of thirty pieces of silver. The contrast is stark.

When compared to the betrayal we experience in our lives—our tears, our shattered dreams, and even the trauma of lives that may seem on the verge of ruin—our betrayal seems less significant. As with Joseph, God uses life experiences like betrayal to shape us, to strengthen us to live out the purpose he has for our lives. Although

God does not create evil, I believe he can and does use evil for good purpose.[2]

Jesus endured the ultimate betrayal to give us the life God has planned for us. He will help us endure betrayal in our own lives. When we come to him in prayer, weary from our anguish, he will help us move beyond it. He will give us rest to strengthen us to live out his purpose for our lives.[3]

Prayer

Lord Jesus,

I feel betrayed. (Describe the situation and the pain you are feeling as a result.) I know I can't change the past. Please help me. Give me relief from the anguish of my pain. Give me rest from the constant torment of my thoughts. Help me feel your presence. I trust you will rescue me from the turmoil of this betrayal. I plead for strength of faith to live out your purpose for my life. Amen

Questions to Consider

- Can you imagine the terror Joseph's bothers must have felt when they became aware that they were at the mercy of the brother they had sold as a slave?

- How did Joseph understand this situation as God's plan?

- How might Judas have felt when Jesus acknowledged his betrayal?

- Why do you think betrayal is experienced as so deeply wounding—even life altering?

- Is Jesus calling you to turn to him to heal you from the damage of betrayal?

๛THIRTEEN๛

A Prayer at Easter

Scripture

<u>Old Testament</u>   Suggested reading: Isaiah 53

But he was pierced for our transgressions,
      he was crushed for our iniquities;
the punishment that brought us peace was upon him,
      and by his wounds we are healed.
We all, like sheep, have gone astray,
      each of us has turned to his own way;
and the Lord has laid on him
      the iniquity of us all.
After the suffering of his soul,
      he will see the light of life and be satisfied;
by his knowledge my righteous servant will justify many,
      and he will bear their iniquities. (Isaiah 53:5, 6, 11)

<u>New Testament</u>   Suggested reading: Mathew 28:1-10; Mark 16:1-8;
                   Luke 24:1-12; John 20:1-18

On the first day of the week, very early in the morning, the women took the spices they had prepared and went to the tomb. They found the stone rolled away from the tomb, but when they entered, they did not find the body of the Lord Jesus. While they were wondering about this, suddenly two men in clothes that gleamed like lightning stood beside them. In their fright the women bowed down with their faces to the ground, but the men said to them, "Why do you look for the living among the dead? He is not here; he has risen! Remember how he told you, while he was still with you in Galilee 'The Son of Man must be delivered into the hands of sinful men, be crucified and on the third day be raised again.' " Then they remembered his words. (Luke 24:1-8)

What does this Scripture mean to me?

As Isaiah prophesied the birth of the Messiah, so he also foretold the death and resurrection of Christ centuries before his crucifixion. Isaiah wrote with powerful imagery using words like "pierced" and "crushed". These words described visions he received from God. Jesus would be tortured and crushed with the weight of our sins for, "We all, like sheep have gone astray." He would be the sacrifice to intercede for all of us. Still, the words from Isaiah brought hope with this prophesy of death and suffering when he described the resurrection as "...the light of life." It wasn't enough for Jesus to die a cruel death. The miracle of Easter was his resurrection.

It's this miracle that his friends encountered when they visited the tomb of Jesus at dawn on the third day after the horror began that must have seemed like the beginning of the end. They had witnessed the suffering of his crucifixion and stood powerless in the shadow of the cross as he died. They were grieving when they came upon the empty tomb with the stone rolled away from its entrance. Little wonder that they were afraid of the men dressed in gleaming clothing as they were told, "...he is risen!"

When the women hurried to tell the apostles of their discovery, their story was so improbable, we are told it was dismissed as nonsense![1] They couldn't understand what had happened until Jesus himself made appearances to them soon afterward. Although the Scripture quoted here is from the Gospel of Luke, all four Gospels record similar descriptions of that first Easter morning.

Those early followers of Jesus lived through the trauma of his crucifixion and their discovery of the supernatural event of his resurrection. They didn't have the perspective of almost 2,000 years of Easter Sundays with books, sermons, and hymns to help them understand the significance of the resurrection. The terror of one weekend in their lives brought one bright morning that has changed the course of human existence forever. The events of that morning provided them and us with the hope of new life.

It was my sin and yours that pierced and crushed the man known as Jesus. It was the miracle of his resurrection as God's Son that provides us with his grace.

Prayer

Lord Jesus,

Forgive me for the sins that pierced and crushed you. (Ask for forgiveness for the sins that you remember now.) Your presence with me reminds me of the joy of salvation that is mine through you. Help me open my heart to your gifts of forgiveness and love, and the peace you offer to me through my new life in you. I pray for your direction and for strength of faith to use the life and the gifts you have given to me to live in service to you. Amen

Questions to Consider

- How does the context from Isaiah give you a better understanding of the crucifixion and resurrection of Jesus?

- Can you imagine how confused and fearful Jesus' friends might have been after the crucifixion?

- How might people react if the resurrection were to occur today?

- Have you talked about the resurrection of Jesus with those you love?

- How do the people who care about you react to the idea that you truly believe that Jesus is your risen Redeemer?

೮FOURTEEN౪

A Prayer to Accept God's Grace

Scripture

<u>Old Testament</u>   Suggested reading: 1 Samuel 16:1-13;
                                2 Samuel 7:8-28; Psalm 23

The Lord is my shepherd, I shall not be in want.
    He makes me lie down in green pastures,
he leads me beside quiet waters,
    he restores my soul.
He guides me in the paths of righteousness
    for his name's sake.
Even though I walk
    through the valley of the shadow of death,
I will fear no evil,
    for you are with me;
your rod and your staff,
    they comfort me.
You prepare a table before me
    in the presence of my enemies.
You anoint my head with oil;
    my cup overflows.
Surely goodness and love will follow me
    all the days of my life,
and I will dwell in the house of the Lord
    forever. (Psalm 23)

<u>New Testament</u>   Suggested reading: Ephesians 2:1-10

But because of his great love for us, God, who is rich in mercy,
made us alive with Christ even when we were dead in

transgressions—it is by grace you have been saved. And God raised us up with Christ and seated us with him in the heavenly realms of Christ Jesus, in order that in the coming ages he might show the incomparable riches of his grace, expressed in his kindness to us in Christ Jesus. For it is by grace you have been saved, through faith—and this is not from yourselves, it is the gift of God—not by works, so that no one can boast. (Ephesians 2:4-9)

What does this Scripture mean to me?

Psalm 23 is among the best known passages of Scripture. The pastoral images from this poetry of David, the shepherd who became king, are more than beautiful. They are an ardent expression of faith from David, who confidently placed his trust in God to guide and protect him as a shepherd cares for his flock. David knew he didn't deserve God's love but that it was given to him through God's generous gift of grace.

We read in chapter sixteen of 1 Samuel that David, the youngest of Jesse's eight sons, was chosen by God to be anointed by the prophet Samuel as King of Israel. This was not a random choice. As God established his kingdom on earth, he selected a young shepherd with a good heart to lead his people. David understood that God was the sovereign king of Israel and that his own role was to be the shepherd-king, the servant leader of God's chosen people.

God promised David, if he would have complete trust in him, he would guide David to establish a dynasty that would last forever. King David was to be the ancestor of the Shepherd-King God would send to be the Savior of the world. God could and did guide David to lead his people. David trusted him completely even though he was besieged by enemies throughout his reign.

We might contrast David's confident faith with the anxiety we feel in our own lives. While we have challenges to meet on a daily basis, they pale in comparison to the fierce battles, the attempts of assassination on his life, and the responsibility for leadership that King David faced. David knew he was a man who sinned yet he repented, trusting God to forgive him and to be present with him, to guide him, to protect him, to comfort him, to provide for him, and to love him forever.

In the apostle Paul's letter to the Ephesians, Paul calls this grace. He tells us that, even though we sin, God loves us and has provided salvation for us through the resurrection of his Son, Jesus Christ. Paul explains that there is nothing we can do to earn salvation—that it has been given to us as a gift. This is what has been most difficult for me to believe. How can I, knowing the breadth and depth of my sin, expect that eternal salvation has been provided for me?[1] Getting to where I was to accept God's grace was a chasm that I struggled to cross. Rationally, I thought there was something I had to do. I thought I had to force myself to believe: If only I were good enough, if only I would try harder, if only I could believe enough. Finally, there seemed to be no alternative but to let go. I told God I couldn't believe. It was only after that point, that God was able to give me the gift of faith through Jesus Christ.

If you're still struggling, let go. Admit that you can't believe God's promise to you on your own. Open your heart and let God give you his undeserved gift of love. If you've already been able to open your heart to God, he wants to have a real relationship with you. Through prayer, you can talk with him and ask him to help you build your trust in him. I know from personal experience that God will remain with you even during those times when you have trouble feeling like your heart is open. He will not abandon you. This is the relationship you have needed all of your life. Although you may never have understood the concept of grace, God doesn't require you to understand. He requires nothing but letting go of your struggle to remain in control and giving him control of your life.

Prayer

Dear Jesus,

You know that I've struggled to understand your purpose for my life. I've found myself continuing my rational search for meaning in my life only to feel like I'm missing what is most important. Help me give up this search. Help me let go. Help me to open my heart to accept your gift of grace. Help me to receive your gift of faith. Strengthen my faith to have complete trust in you to follow the guidance of your Holy Spirit. Amen

Questions to Consider

- Why do you think David's complete trust in God was so important to his role as king of Israel?

- How do you think David knew that he could have complete trust in God to guide him even when he was aware of his sin?

- Why do you think struggle to understand God's grace through rational thought is so compelling?

- How does this struggle keep us from accepting God's grace?

- How will you know when you have opened your heart to God?

Epilogue: What Have I Learned?

As I was writing the manuscript for this book, I gradually became aware that I was learning more about prayer even as I was writing. As I found my relationship with God deepening and becoming more real to me day-to-day, I realized that prayer was strengthening my relationship with God. I think some, perhaps many, people would describe prayer and God's response to be supernatural, especially since miracles may be almost inevitable. With that thought in mind, it may seem like a paradox that as my talks with God have become more intimate, my relationship with God has felt more relaxed and natural—though I have not lost the sense of awe that surrounds our conversation.

It's been my experience to struggle with confusing theological concepts like the Trinity (i.e., one God in three persons) and worry about how this was different from polytheists who believe in multiple gods.[1] As prayer has strengthened my relationship with God, the presence of the Holy Spirit seems to overcome my efforts to control my concerns about theological concepts as I focus instead on the simple idea of talking with God. Before I was willing to trust God, my prayers were obsessive and ritualistic. God has responded to my pleas for help to trust him with my life. A follower of Jesus, I know that he is God just as the Holy Spirit, who is present with me, is God. I believe God speaks to me through his Holy Spirit and that his Son, Jesus Christ, grants me grace to approach the throne of God, my Father.

I have written these words with confidence and a strong sense that they could be helpful to those who pray reluctantly, feeling intimidated by the mystery of prayer as I was. I have learned that God will help you talk with him. You have only to ask for his help in your own words, trusting him to respond.

Acknowledgments

Having previously published articles in professional journals, I realized that God had given me a gift to write. I had a lingering sense that I was called to write a book. Although I had initiated many previous attempts to write, the words just didn't come to me. I often prayed asking God for help to write a book if it was a part of his mission for my life. One morning, following reading of Scripture, I spontaneously picked up a pad of paper and a pen from the table near my chair and began effortlessly writing an outline for this little book. In the days that followed, the structure and content for the chapters often became clear during my morning meditation, including the Scripture I selected for each of the chapters. I have no doubt that my inspiration for writing was from the Holy Spirit.

I thank my friend, Diana McClintock, for encouraging me to write. To ensure that the content was accurate from a theological framework, I thank Pastor Robyn Bishop, who graciously agreed to review the manuscript; any remaining errors in interpretation of Scripture are mine. Joan Christiansen also reviewed the manuscript to determine its relevance to the mission of Cypress Assistance Ministries. I am indebted to her and to Darrell Christiansen for the opportunity to work with the volunteers, staff, and clients of Operation Jobs.

I thank my parents for bringing me to God through baptism. There are many people in the early years of my faith journey—among them Pastor Ray and Dorothy Haugland—who encouraged me during my teenage years. My brother, Robert, served as God's messenger to bring me back to my faith as an adult after years of forsaking my childhood faith. I thank Lynette Bartel and Pastor Harvey Bongers for giving me opportunities to serve at Messiah Lutheran Church when I returned to the faith. Finally, I thank the members of my Sunday school class at Good Shepherd United Methodist Church for their welcoming friendship.

Notes

Preface

1. John Indermark, Mark A. Thronveit, Thomas P. Long, *Adult Crossings: God's Journey with Us*, Journal, (Inver Grove Heights, Minn: Logos Productions, 2008), 40. This Bible study exposes the violence recorded in the Old Testament to the lens of contemporary thought—especially God's commands to destroy the inhabitants of the Promised Land. I concluded that God's ultimate purpose was to salvage humankind from inevitable sin and that he is powerful and capable of destruction to fulfill his plan for the world he created. As a follower of Jesus Christ, I have accepted that the mystery of God is beyond my understanding.

2. Timothy Keller, *The Reason for God – Belief in an Age of Skepticism* (New York: Dutton, Penguin Group, 2008), 70-86. Keller provides plausible rationale for believing in God, the deity of Jesus Christ, and the infallibility of the Bible.

3. Ibid, 22-34.

4. Jan Karon, *Patches of Godlight* (New York, Penguin Books, 2001). It was Karon's Mitford Years series of novels that awakened me to the meaning of God's grace. Although not a novel in her series of published works, I love this little book with quotations from various sources written as if collected by the main character of the series.

5. Keller, 29, 30.

6. Phillip D. Yancey, *Prayer: Does it Make Any Difference?* (Grand Rapids, Mich: Zondervan, 2006), 48-55. It was Yancey's book that prompted my desire to have dialog (i.e., conversation) with God.

7. Ben Campbell Johnson, *The God Who Speaks: Learning the Language of God* (Grand Rapids, Mich.: Wm B. Eerdmans Publishing Co., 2004), 109-129.

8. Margaret Guenther, *The Practice of Prayer* (Cambridge, Mass.: Cowley Publications, 1998), 41-60.

Introduction

1. Johnson, *The God Who Speaks,* 32-37. Johnson describes the role of the Holy Spirit in GodSpeech.

ONE: A Christmas Prayer

1. John MacArthur, *Prophets, Priests, and Kings* (Nashville: Thomas Nelson, In., 2009), 28, 29. In this Bible Study based on 1 Samuel, MacArthur clearly explains how God allows his people to bear the consequences of their own demands.

2. 1 Samuel 8:6-21.

3. Isaiah 10:20-25.

4. Isaiah 11:1-10.

5. Mathew 1:22, 23.

6. John 19:26, 27. These verses authenticate Jesus' great love for this disciple. While Jesus was near death on the cross, he spoke to his mother and his disciple, John, to ask John to be a son to her.

TWO: A Prayer for Guidance

1. C. S. Lewis, "Nice People or New Men," *Mere Christianity* (New York: HarperCollins Edition, 2001), 207-217. In this essay, Lewis discerns the difference between people who do good and those who are transformed by Christ to live devoted to his service.

THREE: A Prayer for Faith

1. Leviticus 18:21

2.   "What is the significance of the transfiguration of Jesus Christ?" *Transfiguration of Jesus Christ*, 2002-2011, www.allaboutjesuschrist.org /transfiguration-of-jesus-christ.faq.htm (accessed June 11, 2011). Although my personal recollection of the significance of the transfiguration of Jesus was unfocused, this web site explains that it gave his disciples Peter, James, and John a glimpse of the divine nature of Jesus who they had previously only experienced in his human form.

3.   Mark 9:19.

4.   Mark 9:22.

5.   Mark 9:23.

6.   Mark 9:24.

FOUR: *A Prayer for Healing*

1.   2 Kings 18:5, 6.

2.   2 Kings 18:2; 20:6. Hezekiah was age twenty-five when he began his reign of twenty-nine years. In 20:6, we read that fifteen years were added to his life. (My calculation is: 25+29-15=39.)

3.   2 Kings 20:21; 21:1. Hezekiah's son, Manasseh, was born three years after God extended Hezekiah's life by fifteen years.

4.   Leviticus 15:25.

5.   Genesis 1:27.

FIVE: *A Prayer in Time of Grief*

1.   Genesis 1:27.

2.   Genesis 6:9.

3.   John 11:33.

4.   Interpretation of the Holy Spirit as "whispering" to our heart as Jesus grieves with us is mine, undocumented from a theological source.

SIX: A Prayer for Help with Anxiety

1.   1 Kings 3:4-15.

2.   1 Kings 4:29-34.

3.   Ecclesiastes 1:14.

4.   "Ancestors of E=mc²," *Einstein's Big Ideas*, 2005, NOVA: www.pbs.org/wgbh/nova/einstein/ance-m.html (accessed April 17, 2011).

5.   "Life for Survivors after Great East Japan Earthquake and Tsunami of March 11, 2011, *Facts and Details*, http://factsanddetails.com/japan (accessed July 21, 2011).

6.   Mathew 6:34.

SEVEN: A Prayer for Forgiveness

1.   2 Samuel 7:25-29.

2.   Psalm 51 superscription reads: "...A psalm for David. When the prophet Nathan came to him after David had committed adultery with Bathsheba."

3.   Timothy Keller, *The Prodigal God* (New York, Dutton, Penguin Group, 2008). Keller presents a powerful interpretation of the parable known as "The Prodigal Son". His explanation of this Scripture helped me understand God's extravagant gift of grace to me.

EIGHT: A Prayer of Joy

1.   Fleming Rutledge, "Magnificat," *Generous Orthodoxy*, www.generousorthodoxy.org/sermons/a-christmas-sermon-magnificat.aspx (accessed May 14, 2011). Rutledge, one of the first women to be ordained by the Episcopal Church, delivered this sermon about Mary's Magnificat on the third Sunday of Advent, 2010, for Bach Vespers at Holy Trinity Lutheran Church, New York, NY.

2.   1 Samuel 9:15, 16; 10:1. Samuel anointed Saul.

3.   1 Samuel 16:12, 13. Samuel anointed David.

4.   MacArthur, *Prophets, Priests, and Kings*, 57.

5.   Mathew 1:18, 19. After Joseph learned of Mary's pregnancy, he planned to quietly divorce her to avoid exposing her to disgrace.

6.   Luke 1: 41, 42.

NINE: *A Prayer for a Generous Heart*

1.   John 12:8.

2.   www.charitynavigator.org (accessed April 21, 2011). I'm not suggesting that anyone contribute to a specific organization— only that you consider using this website or one of several others available on the internet, as a potential source to identify an organization that you would find worthy of your contributions.

TEN: *A Prayer of Thanks*

1.   Exodus 25:10-22. This passage describes the crafting of the ark of the covenant.

2.   Deuteronomy 10:3-5.

3.   Numbers 4:15. Only descendants of Levi, using the poles inserted through the rings on the ark as described in the above reference from Exodus, were authorized to transport the ark.

4.   MacArthur, *Prophets, Priests, and Kings*, 16-18. MacArthur discusses the Israelites' erosion of their faith in God which led to their decision about the ark recorded in 1 Samuel 4:3.

5.   1 Samuel 5.

6.   1 Chronicles 13:1-14; 14:8-17.

7.   Acts 6:1-5; Acts 7:57-8:1.

8.   Acts 9:1-19; 22:1-21; 26:9-20.

9.   Acts 16:12.

10.   Acts 22:25-29.

11.   Acts 28:28-31.

12.   Acts 28:30-31.

ELEVEN: *A Prayer for Humility*

1.   Isaiah 1:1.
2.   1 Timothy 5:10.
3.   Mathew 16:23-25.

TWELVE: *A Prayer when Feeling Betrayed*

1.   Genesis 37:19.
2.   Romans 8:28
3.   Mathew 11:28.

THIRTEEN: *A Prayer at Easter*

1.   Luke 24:11. Although references to the role of women as leaders in the church are not highlighted in the Gospels, Luke exposes the reaction to the report of the women in this passage— authenticating the importance of their role with his record of their version of the report of Christ's resurrection. It was Mary who was first told that the Messiah was to be born and a group of women who first learned of his resurrection.

FOURTEEN: *A Prayer for Grace*

1.   Phillip D. Yancey, *What's So Amazing about Grace?* (Grand Rapids, Mich.: Zondervan, 1997). For those, like me, who might worry about the depravity of their sin, Yancey describes examples with convincing commentary based on Scripture which gives hope that God really does want to give away his free gift of grace to all who will open their hearts to his Holy Spirit to accept faith in Jesus Christ and sincerely repent of their sins.

Epilogue: *What Have I Learned?*

1.   Lewis, "The Three-Personal God," *Mere Christianity*, 160-165.

About the Author

Patricia Hanson Enmon, known as "Patty" to her family, was baptized in the rural church of her grandparents and raised in a devout Lutheran family. When the faith of her childhood was challenged at a church-sponsored liberal arts college, she began a thirty-six-year search for God which collapsed in atheism. By "coincidence" she was finally able to accept God's grace. After a career as a health care executive spanning three decades, she lives in suburban Houston where she is a member of Good Shepherd United Methodist Church and a volunteer Career Counselor in the Operation Jobs program of Cypress Assistance Ministries.